Yehuda Shenef

Practical Introduction to the Hebrew Script

Learn to read and write Hebrew quickly by using familiar names
and vocabulary already known before the language study,

with tables and easy explanations of Hebrew and Yiddish

Hebrew eye chart

3

Content

Preface

Many people who are willing to learn often lose their interest in the Hebrew language after just a few hours of study, as courses usually require a fairly quick mastery of the letters.

Learning a new language with unfamiliar vocabulary, unknown grammatical rules (and exceptions), linguistic features, etc. the additional problem of being confronted with unidentified letters overwhelms many willing learners and often discourages them immediately.

In doing so, it is mostly overlooked that native-speaking children usually have some lead time to learn the writing of the language they already speak in everyday life.

Over the years I have gotten to know many people who deal with Judaism and Jewish topics in their studies or professionally, but who, despite their affinity to Judaism and the workwise occupation with it, did not manage to overcome the apparently high hurdle. So many only achieved recognizing individual letters of a word or text and ultimately have to be satisfied with it: Christian theologians, guides at Jewish cemeteries and museums, members of Christian-Jewish associations or even German-Israeli societies, genealogists, historians, journalists, Germanists (who deal with "Yiddish" texts), not least as Jews of Russian descent and secular Jews. Almost always the reason was the *difficulty* of getting used to the "strange" letters.

However, timidity, reserve and distance from Hebrew are actually groundless, as there are numerous everyday names such as Joseph, David, Ruth, Michael, Abraham, Elisabeth or Daniel, or commonly known terms such as shalom, amen, Uzi or Hallelujah, or prominent toponyms such as Jerusalem, Bethlehem, Nazareth, Jericho, Haifa, Zion or Israel. Last but not least, there are also many similarities between Hebrew and the writing systems based on Latin letters in

Western languages, as well as numerous common and related vocabulary.

By recourse to words and names that are common and familiar or that can be understood quickly, it is now just as quick and easy to become easily familiar with the Hebrew script and spelling and thus with the Alefbet without tiring cramming of foreign vocabulary and grammar rules. Thus, now it's easy to achieve noticeable learning successes very quickly.

This practical introduction is intended to address precisely this common problem in learning Hebrew and its script. The method is a very simple one, as it is linked to the learner's knowledge, which is most likely *already present before* the language study. The intent learner, who otherwise could be discouraged by umpteen foreign characters, can thus achieve the encouraging success, being able to take recourse to considerable prior knowledge, right from the start. The fairly quick success can only have a positive effect on the further course of the study.

The practical introduction to the Hebrew script can therefore be given as a simple and effective aid as a prerequisite as well as to accompany existing textbooks and courses in the Hebrew language and script. It enables learners of modern Hebrew as well as students of Biblical or medieval Hebrew and Aramaic or Yiddish to have quick access to terrain that is not so completely foreign.

In this sense, good luck to all students and the curious, **mazal tov**.

Yehuda Shenef, Rosh Khodesh Tamuz 5781 ראש חודש תמוז **תשפ"א**

Introduction

Some Required Information About Hebrew

1. The Hebrew script is the basis for the Hebrew, Aramaic and Yiddish (Jewish) languages. The current form of the so-called square script (k'tav meruba) is two and a half thousand years old and is used until today, but differs significantly from the ancient script that was used in earlier Biblical times and which scientifically is termed as paleo-Hebrew. The square script was developed in Babylonia and is the script in the Torah scrolls, Bible prints and the Talmud, as well as medieval works or tombstone inscriptions. The script is also used in contemporary Yiddish and above all Hebrew books and websites in everyday life, although, like in Latin scripts, there are now of course a large number of different script and print types.

2. **The Hebrew script**, unlike the scripts based on Latin and Greek letters, does not run from left to right, but **from right to left**. So, you have to get used to reading the words "backwards", so to speak, starting from the right end of the line.

3. **The Hebrew Alefbet** - named after the first letters Alef and Bet - **consists of 22 letters and 27 characters.**

4. In contrast to the Latin alphabet, the Hebrew alphabet has **no upper or lower case**, but **five** of the **letters at the end of the word take on a different**, elongated **form**. Even if this is unusual, Hebrew only has 27 characters, i.e., only about half that you have to learn with upper and lower case in Latin, Russian, Greek, etc. In Arabic or Persian (almost) all letters change depending on whether they are at the beginning of the word, in the middle or at the end, or individually because not all letters can be connected with others, etc. Compared to this, the Hebrew writing system made up of individual letters is not only refreshingly simple, but actually the simplest in the world.

5. Since every language-writing system inevitably raises problems, Hebrew also has certain peculiarities. As a general rule, **vowels are not notated**. There are many exceptions to this in modern Hebrew. The English word "hand" would be written as "HND" *without* the vowel. This may seem a bit confusing and complicated, of course, but it has become much easier in modern newspaper Hebrew.

In classical texts from biblical or poetic literature, dotted vowel marks are used (similar to the i point, the ü, ö, ä - umlauts in German or Turkish, or the French accented characters é, è or ê, etc.). In other texts, a vowel can sometimes be noted in a word in this way in order to avoid confusion. But that's rare.

This is of course irrelevant for learning to read and write Hebrew letters, as it essentially always depends on conventions that you learn as a matter of course as soon as you are "in the system" or get into it. This is much usually easier than it may sound at first.

The English language also has many conventions that learners have to cope with first. Some diphthongs for example, are pronounced quite differently in many words. Like the "ou" in curi*ou*s, *ou*r or s*ou*l, ... the "u" in t*u*ne or f*u*n, ... the "ow" in h*ow* or c*ow* ... and many more. Why does the "e" in di*e* remain silent ...? Well, even spelled out consonants remain silent: s*w*ord, dou*b*t, *k*nife, su*b*tle, etc. And what is the rule? You have to know. For a beginner, these are considerable difficulties, since the spelling does not provide a reliable indication of the correct pronunciation - for the foreign speaker. Not to mention the spelling of the spoken word!

For someone who is learning English as a foreign language, possibly together with the Latin alphabet, none of this is immediately clear.

Similarly, there are now a number of conventions in Hebrew that one must know and therefore assume. It is not different in any language. Overall, there are only a few of them in Hebrew, so that the Hebrew speaker has the impression of his language that it is spoken as it is written.

7. With a few exceptions, **the pronunciation of Hebrew** - and as good news at the end - **does not cause any problems** with the English-speaking learner, provided that the transcription is correct.

So, there is now no further obstacle. You don't need to consider peculiar nasal sounds or ascending and descending pitches if you wanted to learn Chinese, for example.

The Hebrew Alefbet

Sign	Name	Letter	Pronunciation
א	alef	---	
ב	bet	b, w	
ג	gimmel	g	
ד	dolet	d	
ה	hay	h	emphasized **h**
ו	wof	w	Like English w
ז	zuyn	s	voiced **s**
ח	khet	kh	as in Scot. Loch or German Ba**ch**
ט	tet	t	
י	yood	y	
כ	kof	k, kh	
ך	kof soofit	-kh	
ל	lamed	l	
מ	mam	m	
ם	mam soofit	-m	
נ	noon	n	
ן	noon soofit	-n	
ס	samekh	ss	as in ki**ss**
ע	uyn	---	
פ	pay	p, f	
ף	pay soofit	-f	
צ	tzodi	z, ts	as **ts** in fi**ts**
ץ	tsodi soofit	-ts	
ק	koof	k	
ר	resh	r	
ש	shin	sch, s	
ת	tof	t	

x-*soofit* = Spelling as the *final letter* of a word.

The Hebrew letter names in the table are based on the actual pronunciation. For example, an often read "zayin" is often pronounced in English as "sayin(g)", but in Hebrew as "zuyin" with *uy* as in the word buy.

The Hebrew Alefbet therefore consists of 22 letters and since five of them take a slightly different shape at the end of a word, a total of 27 characters. Since there is no upper or lower case, but only these uniform, constant letters, there is not too much that one has to become familiar with - compared to other languages. Many languages have twice the number of letters with Aa, Bb, ... Gg, etc., whereby one also has to know which words are when to be written in upper or lower case. That is not always clear, for example in the German.

The letters of the Hebrew Alefbet - and whoever feels reminded of the Greek alphabet by the word - is quite right, have their own names that echo the better well-known Greek copies.

In fact, the Greeks took their letter names from Hebrew.

Alef became Alpha
Bet became Beta
Gimmel became Gamma
Dolet became Delta
and so on

Unlike in Greek, the Hebrew names also have a literal meaning.

Alef = beef head
Bet = house
Gimmel = camel
Dolet = gate, door
etc.

As can be seen from the previous table, the Hebrew Alefbet has a few special features. In addition to the final letter forms already mentioned, which occur in five of the twenty-two letters, there are also letters for sounds for which there are no separate characters in English or German. There they are combined in a somewhat complicated way from otherwise differently spoken characters.

Two characters, on the other hand, as mere reading aids, do not have any binding sound equivalent.

With the ש (shin), Hebrew has its own letter for the "sh sound", which is cumbersome in German and is made up of the characters s + h (compare German: s-c-h). Russian has the letter *sha* ш, which, as you can easily see, is borrowed from Hebrew.

The same applies to the kh sound (as in Loch or German Bach), which is also combined only from k + h due to the lack of its own letter. It is represented in Hebrew using the letters ח (khet) or כ (kof, khof), so it even exists twice. In Russian language, this largely corresponds to the letter х (kh), as in Михаил (Mikha'el).

Similarities Between Hebrew Letters

Beginners in Hebrew during reading and writing exercises may have initial problems with the fact that some of the letters look a little bit alike. By comparing the letters that appear similar, we will clarify the differences that exist and sharpen our eyes.

The similarity of some letters shouldn't put anyone off or even despair, since with the Latin script we are using here we are also dealing with characters that someone who is just getting to know them could easily mix up.

Let's take a small m, which differs from a small n only by an additional hook. Compare also the lowercase c and e, which then sometimes appears like an upside-down a. Who could instantly tell a small l (L) from a capital I (i)? We also see the similarities between an O and a Q, the mirroring of q and p, between d and b, etc. They are all letters that, as a newcomer, could and will confuse you, but which do not irritate us any further, since we know them and have internalized the essential details and differences. Like so much in life, that comes with practice and repetition. So, no need to worry.

Anyone who has no trouble in not confusing similar letters like c and e or d and b, has the necessary skills to do the same with a few Hebrew letters that are somewhat similar to one another as well.

At first glance, the letters ב *bet* (b) and כ *kof* (k) appear similar. But juxtaposed, it turns out that the significant difference between the two letters is at the right end of the bottom line. While the kof has an inward curvature, the letter *bet* has here an outward tine. The letter נ *noon* (n) appears here as a bed with shortened lines without any jagged edges.

The letter פ *pay* (p) also bears a certain resemblance to the *bet*, but instead of the straight line at the top, it has an additional small arch that curves inwards to the right.

ב כ נ פ   (modern)

בּ כּ נ פּ   (classic)

The next group of letters with relatively similar and sometimes confusable letters are the characters ה *hay* (h), ח *khet* (kh) and ת *tof* (t).

Again, the striking differences can be determined relatively easily. The *he* differs from the closed *khet* in that it has an opening in the upper left column of the letter, while *tuf* again has a small roof above the left foot and an additional prong at the bottom on the left foot end.

ה ח ת

ה ח ת

The letters ד *dolet* (d) and ר *rash* (r) are often confused. However, the distinction is quite simple. The *dolet* has a sharp point outward at the meeting of the vertical and horizontal lines at the top right. The rash however has the two lines connected by a common arch. One could confuse the final form of the letter *kuff* with both, which looks a bit like a *dolet*, but then has the descender characteristic of all final letters and is therefore quite clearly recognizable, especially since it can actually only appear at the end of one word

ד ר ך

ד ר ך

The letters ג *gimmel*, ו *waf*, ז *zuyin* and the final form of the letter ן *noon* have slight similarities, but here, too, we find clear criteria that make it easy for us to differentiate the characters.

ג ו ז ן

ג ו ז ן

Depending on the font used, the letters ט *tet* (t), ס *samekh* (s) and the final form of the letter ם *mam* (m) appear also somewhat similar. On closer inspection, however, you notice that the *tet*, unlike the *samekh*, is not closed, while this appears o-*like*. The end *mam* also differs from this by its clearly square cube shape. In addition, the letter can only appear at the *end* of a word.

ט ס ם

ט ס ם

The remaining signs of the Hebrew *Alefbet* are quite characteristic,
so (if written neatly) they are hardly confused with others.

ש ק צ ע מ ל י א

ש ק צ ע מ ל י א

As mentioned, some Hebrew letters are also *phonically similar*. In
addition to the previously introduced kh sounds **ח** *khet* and **כ** *kof*,
these are initially the spirants *zuyin*, *samech* and *sin*. While the
zuyin denotes a voiced s-sound, like the z in English, for example in
the word *zoo* or in French *zizanie*, the *samech* corresponds more to
the German s as well as the sign *sin*, which is written in the same
way as the *shin* (= sh).

This is not really bad as it hardly plays a relevant role in practice. If
you mix up one letter or express an s more or less "voiced" as it
should be, it doesn't matter, as you are usually understood that
way anyway. If there is a rare risk of confusion when using shin or
sin, the punctuation helps, which marks the letters therefore: If the
point is at the top left, it is an s-sound and the letter is *sin*, if the
point is at the top right, then it is a sh-sound and a *shin*. If there is
no puncturing, one can confidently assume a sh.

sinn   שׂ – שׁ   *shinn*

As mentioned, the punctuation here is only for a few confusable exceptions that hand down old, historically determined spellings. In English we also use different characters for the same and similar sounds. We have the *s* in *Susan* and the *c* in *Caesar* but the *z* in *Zoo*, the *g* in *genes* or the *j* in *jeans*. We have our *sh* in *shoe*, but we also know the French *j* in jour or the German *ß*, called "es-tzet", which, like in "Straße", reproduces an s-sound as well.

We see that there are peculiarities everywhere and we do not have major problems dealing with them as soon as we are familiar with them. Binding rules always are good to know, but usually there often are some exceptions. Just compare the pronunciation and spelling of words such as *Zeus*, *juice*, *Jews*, *zoos* or *shoes*, etc.

Finally, Hebrew now also has the two t-sounds ט *tet* and ת *tof*, which no longer differ today, but once used to be different dental sounds, similar to the Greek θ theta and τ tau.

Like the Greek θ theta (= t), the Hebrew ת *tof* is unfortunately still often transcribed as "th". Earlier scholars used this th to indicate the respective letters. However, it does not make any practical sense, as the English speaker usually does not care whether a character was written in the original Greek with this or that letter. What's more, it very often causes confusion, as one uses a wrong "th" pronunciation, especially in English.

The two characters א *alef* and ע *uyn* have no equivalent in English. They represent neither vowels nor consonants, but serve as reading or stress aids. In Yiddish, however, these are the vowels: a and e.

Letters as Numbers

The Hebrew Alefbet now offers the learner a special feature that makes it even a little easier to memorize its sequence: **the letters are also numerals**.

One after the other, the Hebrew letters form the numerical values: the units 1-9, then the tens from 10-90 and finally the hundreds from 100 to 400, making a total of 22 letters as digits. With them all other numbers that you need are put together regularly. The process is always gradual. The number 32, for example, consists of 30 and 2, the number 500 is a combination of 400 and 100.

Obviously, you cannot do mathematics with that, for which we use of course the Indian (European) digits that are common worldwide. But keep in mind that there are also Roman numerals that are used internationally (e.g., for years in US films or for numbering in books, etc.). They only have a few characters that need to be combined in a rather complicated way. All other numbers must be formed from only six letters I = 1, V = 5, X = 10, L = 50, C = 100 and M = 1000, whereby it also depends on where the individual letters are placed, because IX gives 9, while XI shows 11.

The Hebrew spelling of numbers by letters can be found today mainly in dates, mostly on Jewish gravestones. Ancient and medieval mystics invested a lot of energy and time in calculating so-called numerical values of words and sentences and, above all, comparing them. Since every Hebrew word consists of letters that also represent a number, the sum of the letters can be added as numbers. The word אדם *adam* (human, person), for example, is numerically noted as 1-4-40, which is why Adam has the "numerical value" 45. The word מה (ma) = "what?" now adds to 45 as well. Mystics now suspected that words with the same numerical value were related to one another.

Perhaps the best-known example of this type of speculation is probably the famous number 666 from the Christian Apocalypse of John, which was written in Greek. Here, too, the Greeks followed the Hebrew example and gave their letters numerical values.

However, the assignment of letters as numbers is undoubtedly a very good learning aid to memorize the order and spelling.

Alef	1		א
Bet	2		ב
Gimmel	3		ג
Dolet	4		ד
Hay	5		ה
Wof	6		ו
Zuyn	7		ז
Khet	8		ח
Tet	9		ט
Yood	10		י
Kof	20	ך	כ
Lamed	30		ל
Mam	40	ם	מ
Noon	50	ן	נ
Samech	60		ס
Uyn	70		ע
Pay	80	ף	פ
Tzodi	90	ץ	צ
Koof	100		ק
Resh	200		ר
Shin	300		ש
Taf	400		ת

Exercise with known (English) first names

In order to become now familiar with the Hebrew script and its application in practice, we will take a look at a few common (not always so) English (but quite common in this country) names in Hebrew spelling. The names are given in Hebrew, as they are printed by default in books, newspapers, on the Internet, etc. The learner can now immediately compare the spellings with the attached Alefbet and thus identify the individual letters and their position in the word.

The list is alphabetical according to the Hebrew.

The diphthong *uy* (as in *buy* or *bye*) at the beginning of a word is איי (alef-yood-yood), otherwise only as יי (yood-yood), comparable to the Dutch *ij* spelling for the same *uy* sound (compare German ei). The W is written with two waf וו - which corresponds exactly to the French *double-vé* and the English *double-u*. An o-sound is often given as alef-waf או. The English **j** (as in John) is transcribed as *g with an apostrophe* = ג' - for example ג'ון (t'shon) = John.

Before we start, I would like to point out once more that Hebrew is written and read **from right to left**.

Edward	אדוארד
Adolf	אדולף
Otto	אוטו
Oliver	אוליבר
Oscar	אוסקר
Iris	איריס
Albert	אלברט
Alexander	אלכסנדר

Angela	אנגלה
Antony, Anthony	אנטוני
Arthur	ארתור

Bob	בוב
Boris	בוריס
Bill	ביל
Barbara	ברברה
Brian	בריאן
Britney	בריטני
Brandon	ברנדון

Julia	ג'וליה
John	ג'ון
George	ג'ורג
Gordon	גורדון
James	ג'יימס
Jim	ג'ים
Graham	גרהם
Grace	גרייס

Donald	דונלד
Dylan	דילן
Dolores	דולורס
Doris	דוריס
Dennis	דניס
Darryl	דריל

Harry	הארי
Henry	הנרי
Heidi	היידי
Hillary	הילארי

Heinz	היינץ
Herbert	הרברט
Harold	הרולד
Hermann	הרמן
Holly	הולי

Vance	ואנס
Winston	וינסטון
Walter	וולטר
Wendy	וונדי
Washington	וושינגטון
Wayne	ויין
Victoria	ויקטוריה
Veronica	ורוניקה

Yuri	יורי
Yasmin	יסמין

Christian	כריסטיאן
Christoph	כריסטוף
Christopher	כריסטופר
Christine	כריסטין

Larry	לארי
Lucy	לוסי
Luke	לוק
Laura	לורה
Leslie	לסלי

Mark	מארק
Maggie	מגי
Mohamed	מוחמד

Mitchell		מיטשל
Milton		מילטון
Michael		מייקל
Mallory		מלורי
Max		מקס
Marjorie		מרג'ורי
Margaret		מרגרט
Martin		מרטין
Mary		מרי
Maria		מריא
Mario		מריו
Matthew		מתיו

Sebastian		סבסטיאן
Steven		סטיבן
Stella		סטלה
Sinclair		סינקלייר
Samira		סמירה
Scarlet		סקרלט

Paul		פאול
Palmer		פאלמר
Pedro		פדרו
Peter		פטר
Patrick		פטריק
Philip		פיליפ
Phoenix		פיניקס
Floyd		פלויד
Pascal		פסקל
Frieda		פרידה
Fritz		פריץ
Francois		פרנסואה
Frank		פרנק
Franklyn		פרנקלין

Karin	קארין
Kobi	קובי
Kevin	קווין
Kate	קייט
Kyle	קייל
Claudia	קלאודיה
Kenny	קני
Carl	קרל
Caroline	קרוליין
Kathleen	קתלין

Robert	רוברט
Rose	רוז
Roland	רולנד
Ronald	רונלד
Roxanne	רוקסן
Rita	ריטה
Rainer	ריינר
Ricky	ריקי

Sean	שון
Seamus	שימוש
Sheldon	שלדון
Shirley	שירלי

Thomas	תומאס
Theodor	תיאודור
Theresa	תרזה

Exercise with known Hebrew first names

Since a number of the letters should already be familiar, we can now start to try it with more well-known Hebrew first names, some of which are so common that one has almost forgotten their origin. There are quite a few of them in English usage, sometimes every day, sometimes less popular, sometimes the original Hebrew form differs a little from the English variant, but that's not a problem. Where there are such deviations, the original Hebrew form is presented in the middle column.

Abraham		אברהם
Adam		אדם
Aaron	a*H*aron	אהרון
Job	ee-yow	איוב
Elia	el-yahu	אליה
Elisabeth	eli-*shewa*	אלישבע
Eliezer		אליעזר
Esther		אסתר
Ephraim		אפרים
Ariel		אריאל

Ben		בן
Benjamin	b*i*nyamin	בנימין
Baruch	ba-rookh	ברוך

Gabriel		גבריאל
Gabi		גבי
Gabor	g*i*bor	גיבור

Deborah	d'*w*ora	דבורה
David		דוד
Dan		דן
Dina		דינה

Danny, Dani		דני
Daniel		דניאל

Abel	*ha 'w*el	הבל
Hosea	ho*sh*ea	הושע

Zachary	*z*ekhar-*ya*	זכריה

Eve	*kha*-wa	חוה
Chaim	khuym	חיים
Anna, Hanna	*kh*ana	חנה

Toby	to*w*-*y*a	טוביה

Juda/s	y*e-h*oo-da	יהודה
Judith	ye-hoo-dit	יהודית
Jehoshua		יהושע
Joachim		יואכים
John	yo-*kha*n*an*	יוחנן
Josef, Joseph		יוסף
Jacob	y*a'a*kow	יעקב
Isaac	yi*tz-kh*ak	יצחק
Jeremiah	*yir-me-ya-hu*	ירמיהו
Joshua	yo-*sh*ua	יושע
Ismael	*yish*-ma-el	ישמעאל
Israel	*y*is-ra-el	ישראל

Cohen, Cohn		כהן
Caleb		כלב

Leah		לאה

Levi		לוי
Laila		ליילה
Lilith		לילית

Magdalena		מגדלנה
Micha	me-kha	מיכה
Michael	me-kha-el	מיכאל
Menasse	mena-*she*	מנשה
Mordechai	mor-de-khay	מרדכי
Miriam	mir-yam	מרים
Moses	mo-*shay*	משה
Matthias	ma-*tit*-ja	מתתיה

Noah	no-a*kh*	נח
Nahum	na-*kh*um	נחום
Naomi		נעמי
Nathan	no-tan	נתן

Amos		עמוס
Emanuel	*im*-anu-el	עמנואל

Ruben	roo-*we*n	ראובן
Rebecca	*riw*ka	רבקה
Ruth		רות
Rahel, Rachel	ra*kh*el	רחל
Rafael		רפאל

Saul	*sha*-ool	שאול
Sulamith	*shoo*-la-mit	שולמית
Salome	*sha*-lo-me	שלומה
Salomon	*shlo*-mo	שלמה
Salman		שלמן

Susan	*sho*-*sha*-na	שושנה
Samuel	*shmoo*-el	שמואל
Simon	*shi*-mon	שמעון
Samson	*shi*m-*sho*n	שמשון
Sarah		שרה

| Tamar/a | | תמר, תמרה |

Exercise with geographical names

To become more familiar with the Hebrew letters, let's next look at some well-known geographic names that are (largely) the same in the English and Hebrew languages. Where there are discrepancies in pronunciation, this is shown again in the middle column.

Uganda		אוגנדה
Augsburg		אוגסבורג
Austria	*ostria*	אוסטריה
Australia	*ostralia*	אוסטרליה
Uruguay		אורוגוואי
Izmir		אזמיר
Atlanta		אטלנטה
Iowa		איווה
Italia	*italia*	איטליה
Indianapolis		אינדיאנפוליס
Europe	*ay*-ro-pa	אירופה
Istanbul		איסטנבול
Iran		איראן
Albuquerque		אלבוקרקי
England	*angliya*	אנגליה
America		אמריקה

Asia	asi-ya	אסיה
Africa		אפריקה
Athens	a-*tu*-na	אתונה

Baghdad		בגדאד
Bavaria	ba-*war*-*ia*	בוואריה
Bohemia	bo-*he*-m*ia*	בוהמיה
Boston		בוסטון
Burkina Faso		בורקינה פאסו
Belgium	bel-giya	בלגיה
Brasilia	bra-sil	ברזיל
Brussels	br*ee*-sel	בריסל
Brisbane		בריסביין
Barcelona	bar-*tze*-lo-na	ברצלונה
Berlin		ברלין

Guatemala		גואטמלה
Georgia	georgi*ya*	גיאורגיה
Glasgow		גלזגו
Germany	*gher*-man-*ya*	גרמניה

Dallas		דאלאס
Detroit		דטרויט
Danube	*danuba*	דנובה
Denmark		דנמרק

Hanoi		האנוי
Hawaii		הוואי
Havana		הוואנה
Hollywood		הוליווד
Hong Kong		הונג קונג
Honduras		הונדורס

Heidelberg		היידלברג
Hiroshima		הירושימה
Hamburg		המבורג
Hannover		הנובר

Wellington		וולינגטון
Washington		וושינגטון
Vatican		ותיקן
Taiwan		טייוואן
Wuhan		ווהאן
Vienna	wi-n*a*	וינה
Utah	yoo-ta	יוטה
Houston	yoo-ston	יוסטון
Venice	way-ne-*tziya*	ונציה
Geneva		ז'נבה

Kuwait	koo-w*ai*t	כווית
Calcutta		כלכותה

Las Vegas		לאס וגאס
Lebanon	*Le*-**w**a-non	לבנון
London		לונדון
Latvia		לטביה
Liverpool		ליברפול
Leeds		לידס
Leipzig		לייפציג
Lichtenstein		ליכטנשטיין

Mainz	ma-**ge**n-za	מגנצה
Madrid		מדריד
Montreal		מונטריאול
Moscow	mos-**kw**a	מוסקבה

Mississippi		מיסיסיפי
Mecca		מכה
Melbourne		מלבורן
Milwaukee		מילווקי
Mexico		מקסיקו

Norway	norweg*iya*	נורבגיה
Nuremberg	N*i*rn-berg	נירנברג
New York		ניו יורק
Newcastle		ניוקאסל
Nepal		נפאל

Syria	s*oo*r-ya	סוריה
Siberia	sl-beer	סיביר
Sidney		סידני

Iraq		עיראק

Poland	po-l*i*n	פולין
Phoenix	*fee*-niks	פיניקס
Florence	*fee*-ren-*tz*e	פירנצה
Panama		פנמה
Prague		פראג
Pretoria		פרטוריה

Zürich	*zi*-rich	צידיך

Kabul		קאבול
Quebec	*kwee*-bek	קוויבק
Connecticut		קונטיקט
Kosovo		קוסובו

Qatar		קטאר
California		קליפורניה
Kiev	ki-**yew**	קייב
Calgary		קלגרי
Canada		קנדה

Ruanda		רואנדה
Rome	rom*a*	רומא
Russia	roo-si-ya	רוסיה
Rio de Janeiro		ריו דה ז'נרו
Sweden	Swe-di-ya	שוודיה
Stuttgart		שטוטגרט
Chicago	**shi**-ka-go	שיקגו

A few names of countries in Hebrew deviate completely from forms common today. They derive from biblical or Talmudic sources that are (far) older than today's naming, which often have their origins at best in medieval times.

India	*ho-du*	הודו
Greece (Ionia)	*yo-won*	יוון
Libya	*loow*	לוב
Egypt	*mitz-ra-yim*	מצרים
China	*sin*	סין
Spain	*s'fa-rad*	ספרד
France	*tzar-fat*	צרפת
Cyprus	*ka-fri-sin*	קפריסין
Yemen	*tay-man*	תימן

Exercise with Biblical Toponyms

Let us return to more familiar territory. Due to the popularity of the Bible and the media coverage of the so-called Middle East, many geographical and historical names from Israel and its history are generally known, although here too there are occasional minor or more serious deviations.

Emmaus		אמאוס
Ashdod		אשדוד
Assyria		אשור
Ashkelon		אשקלון

Beersheba	bear-shay-**wa**	באר שבע
Babylon	ba-**wee**-lon	בבילון
Babel	ba-**w**el	בבל
Bethel, Beth El	be**t**-el	בית אל
Bethlehem	be**t**-le**kh**em	בית לחם
Bethania	bet anee-ya	בתניה
Betar		ביתר
Bet Shemesh		בית שמש

Gadera		גדרה
Galilee	*ga-lil*	גליל
Jenin		ג'נין
Gethsemane	g**a**t-**sh**ma-n**im**	גת שמנים

Deganya	De-gan-ya (a kibbutz)	דגניה
Damascus	da-ma-s**ek**	דמשק

Mount Herzl	har-hertzel	הר הרצל
Mount Carmel	har-ha-kar-mel	הר הכרמל
Armageddon	har-meggido	הר מגידו

Mount Sinai	har-sin*uy*	הר סיני
Mount Zion	har-**tz**ee-yon	הר ציון
Herzliya	Hertz-li-ya	הרצליה
Mount Tabor	har-tabor	הר תבור

Hebron	***kh*ew-ron**	חברון
Hadera	***kh*adera**	חדרה
Hazor	***kh*asor**	חצור
Haifa	***Kh*ay-fa**	חיפה
Aleppo	***kh*a-lef**	חאלב

Tiberias	tee-**w**er-ya	טבריה
Tulkarem	tul karem	טול כרם

Jawne	Yaf-ne	יבנה
Yad Vashem		יד ושם
Judea	ye-hu-da	יהודה
Jaffa	ya-fo	יפו
Jordan	y*a*r-den	ירדן
Jerusalem	*ye-roo-sha-lo-yim*	ירושלים
Jericho	yay-ree-kho	ירחו
Israel	***y*is-ro-el**	ישראל

Genezareth	***ki*-ner-et**	כנרת
Kfar Hanna	*k'far* <u>**kh**</u>ana	כפר חנה
Kapernaum	*k'far* na**kh**um	כפר נחום
Carmel		כרמל

Lod (Lydda)	*lod*	לוד

Megiddo		מגידו

English	Pronunciation	Hebrew
Mamre		ממרא
Masada	ma-*ts*a-da	מצדה

English	Pronunciation	Hebrew
Nazareth	notz-r*at*	נצרת

English	Pronunciation	Hebrew
Sodom	*sd*om	סדום
Sinai	See-n*uy*	סיני

English	Pronunciation	Hebrew
Gaza	*a-s*a	עזה
En Gedi		עין גדי
Akko		עכו
Gomorrah	*a*-mo-ra	עמורה
Amman		עמאן
Afula		עפולה

English	Pronunciation	Hebrew
Persia	*paras*	פרס
Euphrates	*frat*	פרת
Petach Tikvah	pay-takh tee-qua	פתח תקוה

English	Pronunciation	Hebrew
Caesarea	kay-sar-*ya*	קיסריה

English	Pronunciation	Hebrew
Ramat Gan		רמת גן

English	Pronunciation	Hebrew
Samaria	*sho*m-r*on*	שומרון
Sichem (Nablus)	*shay*-khem	שכם

English	Pronunciation	Hebrew
Tabor		תבור
Tel Aviv		תל אביב

Exercise with internationally used foreign words

The list of vocabulary known to you even before starting a Hebrew language course is by no means exhausted with geographical and personal names. There are also a large number of foreign words in international use that have found their way into almost all languages and thus naturally also into modern Hebrew. So, in order to get used to reading (and writing) the Hebrew script even more, we will look at a small selection for practice. Some only differ in the word ending, as they rarely came into Hebrew through English.

Evolution	ay-wo-loo-*tzia*	אבולוציה
Egoism		אגואיזם
Ozon		אוזון
Utopia	oo-to-pee-ya	אוטופיה
Etymology	et*i*molog*ia*	אטימולוגיה
Inflation	infla-*tz-ya*	אינפלציה
Atheism		אתאיזם

Beer	bir*a*	בירה
Bank (institute)		בנק
Bronchitis		ברונכיטיס

Genetic	genetic	גנטיקה
Globe	glo-boos	גלובוס
Graphic	grafik*a*	גרפיקה

Discus		דיסקוס
Discotheque		דיסקוטק
Drama		דרמה

Humor		הומור
Hormone		הורמון
Harmony	Harmon*ia*	הרמוניה

Visa	vee-sa	ויזה
Veto		וטו
Waltz	wa*ls*	ולס

Type	tee-pos	טיפוס
Tactic	ta*khsis*	טכסיס
Tenor		טנור
Zenith	say-ni*t*	זֶנִית

Alcohol	*ko-ho*l	כוהל
Chlorine	klor	כלור

Lyric	*lirika*	ליריקה
Lexicon		לקסיקון

Mania		מאניה
Magnet		מגנט
Million	mil-yon	מיליון
Monolog		מונולוג
Muslim	muslim*i*	מוסלמי
Mantra		מנטרה

Satire	satir*a*	סאטירה
Soya		סויה
Socialism		סוציאליזם
Statistics	statis-tee-ka	סטטיסטיקה
Sisyphus	si-si-fos	סיזיפוס

Symptom		סימפטום
Seminar		סמינר
Sarcasm		סרקזם

Phobia		פוביה
Planet	planet*a*	פלנטה
Provocateur	pro-wo-ka-t*or*	פרובוקטור
Prose	pro-saw	פרוזה
Project	pro-yekt	פרויקט
Principle	prin-tzip	פרינציפ
Paranoia		פרנויה

Casino		קזינו
Kiosk		קיוסק
Kangaroo		קנגורו

Revue	rew-*yu*	רביו
Radio		רדיו
Roman		רומן
Rosemary	roz-ma-reen	רוזמרין
relevant	re-le-van-ti	רלוונטי
Republic	re-publi-k*a*	רפובליקה
Reflex	ray-fleks	רפלקס
Recipe	ray-tzept	רצפט

Some already known Hebrew terms

Abba (father)	(Aramaic)	אבא
EL-AL	(Israeli airline)	אל על
Amen	(= „okay")	אמן
Elohim	(god)	אלוהים

Hallelujah		הללויה

Chanukah	(Light-Festival of inauguration)	חנוכה

Klezmer		כלי זמר
Knesset	(Israeli Parliament)	כנסת
Cherub	*kroow*	כרוב
kosher	k*a*sher	כשר

Megillah	(scroll)	מגילה
Midrash	(exegesis)	מדרש
Moloch		מולוך
Mossad	(„the" institute)	מוסד
Mezuzah		מזוזה
Maccabi		מכבי
Mammon	(property)	ממון
Menorah	(glower)	מנורה

Sukkot	(Feast of Booths)	סוכות

Uzi (weapon)	oo-**see**	עוזי

Purim	(holiday)	פורים
Passover	pay-sakh	פסח

Kaddish	(prayer)	קדיש
Kibbutz	(settlement)	קיבוץ

Shabbat	(weekly resting day)	שבת
shalom	(greeting: peace)	שלום
Shekel	(Israeli currency)	שקל

Tora	Commandments by God	תורה
Talmud	schooling	תלמוד

מִי

יכול לקרוא,

יש היתרון

Reading Yiddish Texts

In addition to Hebrew and Aramaic, the Hebrew Alefbet is mainly used to write the Yiddish language. The peculiarity here (perhaps an advantage) is that in Yiddish, differently than in the so-called Semitic languages, vowels are spelled out - insofar as they are not Aramaic or Hebrew foreign words. The disadvantage for the beginner is that spoken Yiddish can differ considerably from written Yiddish, all the more because Yiddish has many dialects. Of course, this does not come as a surprise when you consider that the former language area of Yiddish stretched from Alsace to almost the Urals, making it the most widely spoken language in Europe. For example, the name Moshe (Moses) was spoken mow-sha in Western Europe, but Moy-sha in Eastern Europe. As in Swiss German, this had little or no effect on the spelling. For anyone who wants to deal with the Hebrew Alefbet, it is definitely a good exercise to also delve into Yiddish a bit, also in order to be able to distinguish between different languages that are notated in the Hebrew script.

Since Yiddish is basically a Germanic language like English, there are more in common than one would like to believe at a distance. And those who already speak some German have the advantage that there is a larger common vocabulary. This is because Yiddish and modern New High German developed in parallel from Middle High German.

The Seven Vowels in Yiddish

In Yiddish there are now seven vowels which, as already mentioned, are written out with letters. So, let's see how they are recorded in detail. The alef א serves as a letter for two - admittedly differently marked - vowels, like the German umlauts that turn an o into an ö.

A = אַ   (as u in fun)

The letter Alef, under which there is a small horizontal line, is used to reproduce the vowel A.

Example: דאַנק = dank (thanx), זאָגן = sag'n (saying), גאַסט = gast (guest), האַנט = hant (= hand)

O = אָ   (like o in box)

The alef is also used to depict the vowel O, this time underlined too, but clearly distinguishable by the vertical line pointing downwards in the middle of the line.

Example: וואָרט = wort (word), נאָדל = nodl (= needle), נאָז = nos (= nose)

U = ו   (like u in Susan or oo in tool)

With the letter Waw ו the vowel U is notated in Yiddish. However, a double וו does not express a vowel, but as already explained the W, an influence that incidentally has been carried over from Yiddish into modern Hebrew when transcribing foreign words and names. If the U is at the beginning of the word, the ו is preceded by an alef, otherwise the character would have to be read as a V.

Example: בוך = bookh (book), און = oon (= and), זוכן = such'n (seek)

I = י (like i in window or ee in bee)

The vowel i is represented by the Hebrew letter yood. If the vowel is at the beginning of the word, an alef is put in front again here, as otherwise one would have to read a y instead of an i.

<u>For instance</u>: די = dee (the), בילד = bild (picture), ביר = beer, אין = in, איך = ich (= I, me), קינד = Kind (child)

E = ע (like ay in say or e in begin)

The vowel E is always represented with the letter uyn.

<u>Examples</u>: דער = der (the), נעמען = nemen (= take), בעט = bet (= bed)

Diphthongs:

They are sometimes extremely complicated for English learners (who also have to *write* the language) because the same sound can be written in quite different ways.

If, for instance, we take the following words: *break, take, way, rain, weight, ...* so there are five different spellings for one sound which is linguistically notated as: **/ eɪ /**. Actually, that is not really an exception. How about *blow, moan, though* (= **/ əʊ /**) or beer, pier, pear (= **/ ɪə /**) or loud and cow ... whereby a *certain* spelling is spoken very differently: *loud* or *soul* - *blow* or *how*, etc. And we haven't even considered regional accents and dialects. In Brooklyn borough for instance, the dog becomes a "dawg" and so on ... Binding rules? No chance, forget about it.

OY – OI = וי

Where English has two variants, in Yiddish there is always waf-yood
וי, unless it is the beginning of the word where an alef is placed in
front of it, as otherwise one would have to read vi.

Examples: לויפער = loifer (runner), אויף = oif (up, upon), טויזנט =
toisent (thousand)

AI, AY, EI, EY = יי

To paraphrase the many "uy" (I, buy, bye, …) spellings, Yiddish has
the *double yood* יי, which, as already mentioned, is made up of two
ii, similar to the *ij* in Dutch. Exceptions are words in which a double
ii must be read as yi, such as in יינגל = yingl (boy).

In fact, this is not a real exception to the rule, but a negligence, as
the single i-point, which usually indicates the ee-sound in dotted
Hebrew texts, is omitted.

In the same way, in some spellings, instead of Yiddish you can see
"idish", but this spelling has not become generally accepted. Again,
an alef is used here initially as איי.

Examples: מייל = mile, טייג = tuyg (dough), צייט = tzuyt (time), איינס
= uyns (one), אייז = ice

Yiddish Reading Exercise

Since the consonants are now somewhat familiar to us and they are usually spoken as in German, we can now look at a few Yiddish vocabulary - with vowels written out. Naturally, our selection only has terms that are at least similar in English. There are of course a lot of terms where this is not the case, but some however are popular in English as well.

August	ow-goo-st	אוגוסט
automobile	o-to-mo-beel	אוטאָמאָביל
Ice		אייז
Islam		איסלאם
old	alt	אלט
all	a-lay	אלע
anarchism	-kh-	אנאַרכיזם
Bagel		בייגל
Breast	broost	ברוסט
good	goot	גוט
December	day-tzem-ber	דעצעמבער
House	hoyz	הויז
home	huym	היים
Hallo, hello	hello	העלא
Day	tog	טאָג
Dance	ton-tzen	טאַנצן
Year	yor	יאָר
Light	leekht	ליכט
Milk	milkh	מילך
Night	nokht	נאַכט
Earth	aired	ערד
Fish		פיש
Pedal	pay-dal	פעדאַל
Pelican		פעליקאַן
Cement	tzay-ment	צעמענט

come	koom	קום
right		ריכטיק
Sweat	shwuys	שווייס
Shoe	shukh	שוך
School, Synagogue	shool	שול
(ho)spital	shpee-tal	שפּיטאַל

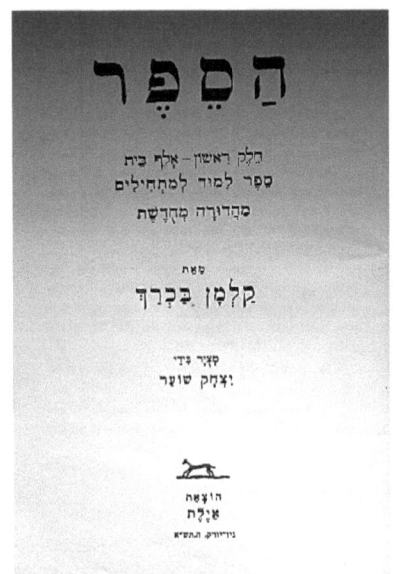

Sefer Alef Bet – a textbook by *Kalman Bacherach*, New York 1941, with which my father Eliyahu learned Hebrew

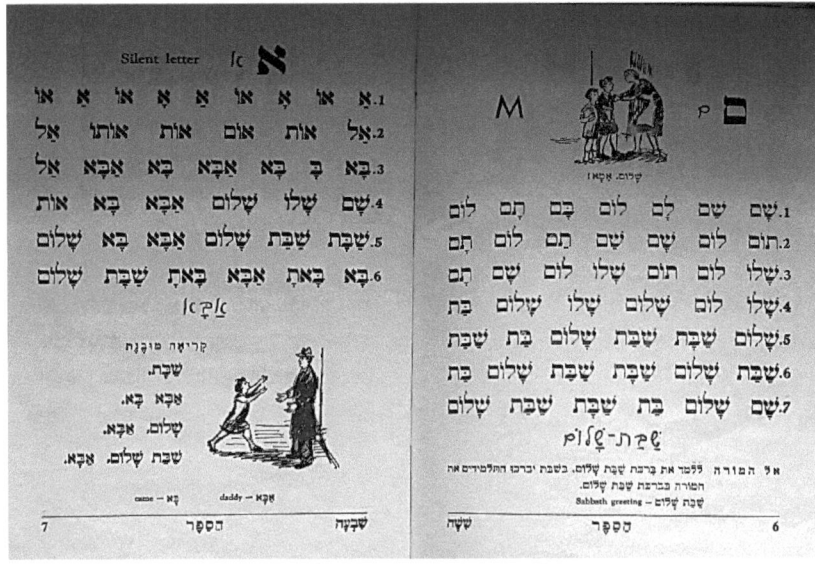

קלמן בכרך - ספר אלף-בית

Recognizing Different Languages in Hebrew Script

Anyone who has followed the exercises so far will be able to cope with the Hebrew script to some extent. Perhaps good enough meanwhile to tell whether a text in Hebrew letters is Yiddish, Aramaic or Hebrew.

Very different languages are written in the Latin script and if you are sufficiently familiar with it, you can usually tell very quickly whether it is a Finnish, Spanish, Turkish, English, German or Latin text.

Why is this? Because every language has its characteristic features such as upper and lower case, umlauts, additional letters and the like.

Since you are generally familiar with it, you can usually recognize the languages straight away. Wouldn't it be good to do the same with languages written in Hebrew letters?

Let's look at three short texts and their spellings and characteristics in order to determine which language it is based on distinctive peculiarities.

Text 1:

אלה הדברים אשר דבר משה אל כל ישראל בעבר הירדן במדבר
בערבה מול סוף בין פארן ובין תפל ולבן וחצרת ודי זהב

Text 2

אלין פתגמיא די מליל משה עם כל ישראל בעברא דירדנא אוכח
יתהון על דחבו במדברא לקבל ים סוף בפארן דאתפל על מנא
ובחצרות דארניזו על בשרא ועל דעבדו דדהב

Text 3

דאָס זײַנען די ווערטער וואָס משה האָט גערעדט צו גאַנץ ישראל
אויף יענער זײַט פון ירדן אין דער מדבר אין דעם פלוין
קעגענאיבער דעם ים סוף צווישען פארן אונד צווישען תופל
אונד לבן אונד חצורות אונד די זהב

All three texts have the first verse of the fifth book of Moses, which Christian theologians name "Deuteronomy" and which in Jewish tradition is called ספר דברים (sefer dwarim).

In a direct comparison of the three verses, you will notice that the first text is significantly shorter than the other two. That is the Hebrew text. The second is the Aramaic and the last text is the Yiddish translation of the same Bible verse.

The Hebrew text just takes 22 words and 81 letters, the Aramaic 29 words and 116 letters, while the Yiddish text takes 38 words and 162 letters. The English translation of the King James Bible takes 31 words and 139 letters. So, the original Hebrew text is much shorter and requires significantly fewer characters.

If we take a closer look at the texts, we can see that the majority of Hebrew words with two, three, four or five letters are relatively short. Aramaic is already a lot longer.

The letter alef א, which is often found at the end of a word, is a characteristic feature in the appearance of the language, and rather rarely used in Hebrew.

In the above text we have Hebrew במדבר (ba'midbar = in the desert) and the same in Aramaic as במדברא (ba'madbra).

Yiddish is almost twice as long - as the length of individual words - because it spells out the vowels. The א with the sublines אַ אָ and the frequent uyn ע as a paraphrase for the e-sound (which is also very common in the German language) are very typical of Yiddish. Combinations such as אוי (oi) or איי (ai), which can rarely occur in other languages, are also striking.

So Hebrew, Yiddish and Aramaic can be relatively easily differentiated in the way they appear. This of course is quite helpful because every now and then words from the other languages appear in a text. For instance, there are many Hebrew words in Yiddish. Now you know, they usually are shorter and have no written vowels.

In English, too, it is common to integrate Greek words whose origin is marked by a y instead of an i, by a ph instead of an f, e.g., both in the word physics (*fee-seek*), or to integrate French terms with accent marks and the like.

The Development of the Hebrew Alefbet

Name of the Letter	Paleo-Hebrew	Classical Square Script	Common Handwriting	Modern Type
Alef	✦	א	לc	א
Bet	⟩	ב	⟩	ב
Gimmel	⋀	ג	⟨	ג
Dolet	◢	ד	⟩	ד
He	⧧	ה	⟩	ה
Waf	Y	ו	/	ו
Suyn	I	ז	⟩	ז
Chet	日	ח	⟨	ח
Tet	⊗	ט	⟨	ט
Yood	⟲	י	'	׳
Kaff	⟩	כ	⟩	כ
Lamed	⟨	ל	⟨	ל
Mam	⟲	מ	N	מ
Noon	⟲	נ	⟩	נ
Samech	⟊	ס	O	ס
Uyn	O	ע	⟳	ע
Pay	⟩	פ	⟳	פ
Tzadi	⟲	צ	3	צ
Koof	Φ	ק	⟩	ק
Resh	◁	ר	⟳	ר
Shinn	W	ש	ℓ	ש
Taf	✕	ת	⟳	ת

A little Hebrew at the End

Or to *begin* with … Preferably with a good Hebrew course. As for many other languages, there is a whole range of very good ones on YouTube that are free of charge. It is best not to limit yourself to one source when learning a language, since the spoken language will also be spoken to and by different people and read by different authors and speakers. Just try Google in Hebrew or any topic on the Hebrew or Yiddish Wikipedia page.

Hebrew language courses are in many cases expensive, clumsy, and sometimes cumbersome in the attempt to be over-correct.

So here are a few more Hebrew words. To start …

ברכה ושלום מזל טוב.

Student	talmid	תלמיד
Schooling	talmud	תלמוד
Book	sefer	ספר
language	safa	שפה
I	a-ni	אני
I am learning (man)	a'ni lo'med	אני לומד
I am learning (woman)	a'ni lo'medet	אני לומדת
Hebrew	eve-reet	עברית
every	coll	כל
Day	yom	יום
every day	coll yom	כל יום
good	tov	טוב
I am a good student	a'ni talmid tov	אני תלמיד טוב
same, female	a'ni talmida to'va	אני תלמידה טובה
The book is good	ha-sefer tow	הספר טוב
fast	ma-hair	מהר

I am learning fast	a'ni lomed ma-her	אני לומד מהר
my	she'li	שלי
my book	ha-sefer she-li	הספר שלי
I am reading (man)	a'ni koray	אני קורא
I am reading (woman)	a'ni koraw	אני קורא
I am reading the book	a'ni kore *et* ha-sefer	אני קורא את הספר
I am writing (m.)	a'ni kotev	אני כותב
I am writing (f.)	a'ni kote'wet	אני כותבת
Every day	coll yom	כל יום
Hebrew	eve-reet	עברית
Name	shem	שם
my name = David	shmee do'vid	שמי דוד
my name = Erika	Shmee erika	שמי אריקה
I am from Prague	a'ni mi-prag	אני מפראג
I am from Boston	a'ni mi-boston	אני מבוסטון
Hello, shalom	shalom	שלום
How are you? (to a male)	ma shlom'kha ...?	מה שלומך
How are you? (to a female)	ma schlo'mech ...?	מה שלומך
I am okay	a'ni ba'seder	אני בסדר
thanks	to'da	תודה
many thanks	to'da ra'ba	תודה רבה
All the best!	coll toof	כל טוב
good luck!	ma'zal tof	מזל טוב
good student	talmid tof	תלמיד טוב
Good student (fem.)	talmida to'va	תלמידה טובה
Bye bye	bai bai	ביי ביי

Ancient (Biblical) Hebrew

יﬡﬡ ﬡﬡﬡﬡﬡﬡﬡﬡﬡﬡ

Classical Hebrew Print (k'tav meruba)

אבגדהוזחטי
כדלמםנןסע
פףצץקרשת

Medieval Rashi Script

אבגדהוזחטיכךלמס
נןסעפףלזקרשת

Modern handwriting

שאבגדהוזחי
סעפןמלכיזב
קרשתף

Modern fonts

שלום   שלום   שלום   שלום

שלום   שלום   שלום

שלום   שלום   שלום   שלום

שלום   שלום   שלום   שלום

שְׁמַע יִשְׂרָאֵל יְדֹוָה אֱלֹהֵינוּ יְדֹוָה אֶחָד וְאָהַבְתָּ אֵת
יְדֹוָה אֱלֹהֶיךָ בְּכָל לְבָבְךָ וּבְכָל נַפְשְׁךָ וּבְכָל מְאֹדֶךָ וְהָיוּ
הַדְּבָרִים הָאֵלֶּה אֲשֶׁר אָנֹכִי מְצַוְּךָ הַיּוֹם עַל לְבָבֶךָ וְשִׁנַּנְתָּם
לְבָנֶיךָ וְדִבַּרְתָּ בָּם בְּשִׁבְתְּךָ בְּבֵיתֶךָ וּבְלֶכְתְּךָ בַדֶּרֶךְ
וּבְשָׁכְבְּךָ וּבְקוּמֶךָ וּקְשַׁרְתָּם לְאוֹת עַל יָדֶךָ וְהָיוּ לְטֹטָפֹת
בֵּין עֵינֶיךָ וּכְתַבְתָּם עַל מְזֻזוֹת בֵּיתֶךָ וּבִשְׁעָרֶיךָ
וְהָיָה אִם שָׁמֹעַ תִּשְׁמְעוּ אֶל מִצְוֹתַי אֲשֶׁר אָנֹכִי
מְצַוֶּה אֶתְכֶם הַיּוֹם לְאַהֲבָה אֶת יְדֹוָה אֱלֹהֵיכֶם וּלְעָבְדוֹ
בְּכָל לְבַבְכֶם וּבְכָל נַפְשְׁכֶם וְנָתַתִּי מְטַר אַרְצְכֶם בְּעִתּוֹ
יוֹרֶה וּמַלְקוֹשׁ וְאָסַפְתָּ דְגָנֶךָ וְתִירֹשְׁךָ וְיִצְהָרֶךָ וְנָתַתִּי
עֵשֶׂב בְּשָׂדְךָ לִבְהֶמְתֶּךָ וְאָכַלְתָּ וְשָׂבָעְתָּ הִשָּׁמְרוּ לָכֶם
פֶּן יִפְתֶּה לְבַבְכֶם וְסַרְתֶּם וַעֲבַדְתֶּם אֱלֹהִים אֲחֵרִים
וְהִשְׁתַּחֲוִיתֶם לָהֶם וְחָרָה אַף יְדֹוָה בָּכֶם וְעָצַר אֶת
הַשָּׁמַיִם וְלֹא יִהְיֶה מָטָר וְהָאֲדָמָה לֹא תִתֵּן אֶת יְבוּלָהּ
וַאֲבַדְתֶּם מְהֵרָה מֵעַל הָאָרֶץ הַטֹּבָה אֲשֶׁר יְדֹוָה נֹתֵן לָכֶם
וְשַׂמְתֶּם אֶת דְּבָרַי אֵלֶּה עַל לְבַבְכֶם וְעַל נַפְשְׁכֶם וּקְשַׁרְתֶּם
אֹתָם לְאוֹת עַל יֶדְכֶם וְהָיוּ לְטוֹטָפֹת בֵּין עֵינֵיכֶם וְלִמַּדְתֶּם
אֹתָם אֶת בְּנֵיכֶם לְדַבֵּר בָּם בְּשִׁבְתְּךָ בְּבֵיתֶךָ וּבְלֶכְתְּךָ
בַדֶּרֶךְ וּבְשָׁכְבְּךָ וּבְקוּמֶךָ וּכְתַבְתָּם עַל מְזוּזוֹת בֵּיתֶךָ
וּבִשְׁעָרֶיךָ לְמַעַן יִרְבּוּ יְמֵיכֶם וִימֵי בְנֵיכֶם עַל הָאֲדָמָה
אֲשֶׁר נִשְׁבַּע יְדֹוָה לַאֲבֹתֵיכֶם לָתֵת לָהֶם כִּימֵי הַשָּׁמַיִם
עַל הָאָרֶץ

Mezuzah Text with „Hear Israel "- Prayer

מזוזה עם תפילת שמע ישראל

Some other books by the author:

"The Jews of Hainsfarth: Notes on a former Jewish Community in a Rural Bavarian-Swabian Village", August 2019

„Die Weisheit der Väter: Pirke Awot hebräisch und deutsch, mit Kurzbiographien der zitierten Mischna-Gelehrten", April 2021

„Die Liebe ist der Dichtung Stern: Der Jüdische Friedhof Augsburg Hochfeld: Geschichte, Inschriften, Grabregister, Biographien, Photos (Jewish Cemeteries in Augsburg)", March 2019

„Wann immer ich von Deiner Ehre erzähle ...: Der Augsburger Judenkirchhof - zu Geschichte und Überresten des mittelalterlichen jüdischen Friedhofs in ... Augsburg (Jewish Cemeteries in Augsburg), Dec. 2020

„666 die Zahl des Menschen – das Mysterium der Apokalypse im Spiegel jüdischer Geschichte", Februar 2016

„Karel Capeks Rossum Universal Robots (RUR) – neu übersetzt und aktualisiert", März 2016

„Der jüdische Friedhof von Binswangen, Hintergründe, Fotos, Grabstein-Inschriften, Familiengeschichten / The Jewish Cemetery of Binswangen, Background, Photos, Grave Marker Inscriptions, Family History", (Deutsch + English) Mai 2016

„Der Bundestag zu Augsburg – das Ende des Deutschen Bundes im Sommer 1866", Juli 2016

„Humor, Wucher, Weltverschwörung – die geläufigsten Vorurteile gegenüber Juden und was es mit diesen auf sich hat", March 2017

„Beiträge zur jüdisch-deutschen Sprachgeschichte, mit etymologischem Wörterbuche jüdischer Wörter in der deutschen Hochsprache", 2017

„Mord am Lech, ein jüdisch-bayrischer Kriminalfall aus dem Jahre 1862", 2. Auflage, August 2017

Yehuda Shenef

Practical Introduction to the Hebrew Script

Learn to read and write Hebrew quickly by using familiar names
and vocabulary already known before the language study,

with tables and easy explanations of Hebrew and Yiddish

Printed in Germany

ISBN: 9783754309070

Printed and published by: BoD - Books on Demand, Norderstedt